FRANKLIN & McCLINTOCK

FRANKLIN AND McCLINTOCK

POEMS BY
David West

INTERMEDIA

Some of these poems have appeared previously in:

Alpha
The Canadian Forum
CBC Anthology
The Fiddlehead
Grain
Karaki
Los
Matrix
Nebula
Performance
The Poem Company
Quarry
Salt
The Twelfth Key
Vancouver Co-Op Radio
Waves
The Yarrow Quarterly

Canadian Cataloguing in Publication

West, David S.
  Franklin & McClintock

Poems
ISBN 0-88956-054-4 bd.
ISBN 0-88956-053-6 pa.

I. Title.
PS8595   C811'.5'4   C77-002124-7
PR9199.3

Franklin and McClintock was designed, printed and bound by
Intermedia Press,
Box 3294, Vancouver, B.C., Canada.

Hudson's Bay and Baffin's Bay, from a map dated 1797.

TABLE OF CONTENTS

Franklin

McClintock

Illustrations from **A Narrative of the Discovery of the Fate of Sir John Franklin and His Companions** by Captain Leopold McClintock published in 1860.

LIST OF ILLUSTRATIONS

1
FRANKLIN
1845-1848

TASMANIAN

Sir John Franklin
as governor of
Tasmania
a convict colony
moved with the elite

he felt the heat
same as the transportees
in the camps
felt the heat
of summers
and choked on the dust

extremes of sun
and ice
tanned
his skin

his ships:
pinioned
where manacles
of ice
nipped them tight

and he, grown pale,
was sunk—
his bones
escaped
into the ice

DEPARTURE: 19 MAY 1845

The only photograph of Franklin
was taken
aboard ship the day he left.
It shows him squinting
under the shade
of his cocked-hat,
a telescope furled
under one arm.
He must be
competent
to set out for the north—
he must be,
but looks clumsy,
as only the most
seaworthy men and the best
of ships ever are,
better than they seem.
Snapped like that,
and squeezed
between shutter and lens.

Dreaming of the Pacific
the Admiralty sent
Franklin—Lord, Admiral,
and Governor-General
through the passage
to claim a route
for bulky Indiamen
with billowing sails.

With two ships Terror
and Erebus of the R.N.
and 134 men
they were the largest party
on the ice.
Sure to succeed.
Weather could not stop
men of the empire,
sent by Victoria
to conquer or die
unknowing.

Unsinkable, they were crushed.
Sent to discover, they were lost.

OUT WITH THE TIDE...

Masts stand to the sun
as Terror and Erebus
get under-weigh

spars poke the spooky
harbour mist
where shore-crowds
flutter moonlit pennants
on wind-torn bunting

Jane tearful on shore
blesses them
but her round white face
betrays eye-line traps
that drag at the ships
hauling them back slow

as they sail on
the tide
drags them out

sails full of wind
bend masts of tall pine
toward the ocean
where the long swell
brings with it
echoes of the shoreline

BEFORE THE VOYAGE...

Lady Jane and the southern clime
warmed him up too much.
After the first cold marriage
she spoiled him.
His sterner stuff was melted.
So coming down off the Pacific high,
he prepared for it.

When he knew for certain he was going,
he began the slow process, cooling down.

Three times a day
he took baths in ice
alone in his tub
blue in the face
while icicle thoughts
formed in his mind.

While winter howled outside
he rehashed his trips
to the Arctic shore:
he had deer's meat and fish
tea twice a day (no sugar)
and on Sunday
a cup of chocolate.
Lady Jane never complained
about strange huntsmen
and fishers at the door:
the experience honed his edge
when others died, the diet
turned him out perfectly finished
to sun his sides on the Tasman shore . . .

Waking he found the bath too warm.
When the butler brought more ice,
poured it over him, Franklin
would quite coolly squeeze the sponge
of ice water in his hair,
lather up and shave
while his man held the mirror.

When he drank water,
they couldn't chill it enough.
He was becoming one with the outside.
He adjusted, adapted, his blood slowed
ran chill and deep like northern rivers.
When he breathed, the air melted coming out.
At the intake of breath, sharp explosions
of shattered crystal filled the air.

And at night when Lady Jane
came to his door, it was bolted.
He had re-submerged into his secure dream.
Nothing must interfere
with the process
seeping through his pores.
He was softer than he once was
but better than when he began
steel-bluing himself
tempering the edge of the man.

SHOOTING THE EQUINOX

Franklin crosses the night
above the bergs his mast
pokes thru moon-clouds

later, he notes
the vernal equinox
as the sun rises
he shoots it himself:
a sextant shimmers
in the interstice
of man and ship

FRANKLIN ON THE FOAM

Franklin would often beat back the waves
and howl
as his compass
hit square the pole
and refused to budge
keel lodged in ice

beating a course against
the wind at Trafalgar
he watched the great fall
as the waves slapped
him home again

Franklin beat back the waves
the prow pushing
dark water
into a bow wave
that spread the foam
smooth and white behind

SIR JOHN OF "THE BATH"

In the Atlantic his sailors
rigged a pump over the side
just for him.

While two men worked it
he'd stand with a towel
about his middle
twirling in the spray.

Even on the worst mornings
he'd have his bath on deck.

And when the ships froze
for winter in the north
he still wanted his shower.

He was inured to cold
and hardship.
Yet not even he could dare
with bare-ass the Arctic bath.
He gave it up
when the intake coughed
to a stop
on ice they couldn't chop.

When at last his want weakened him,
he gave in.
Had them melt buckets of ice
and sat in his hottest tub
in forty years,
hoisted high the scrubbing-brush
and began . . .

REPORT

"Having wintered in 1845-6 at Beechey Island after having attempted Wellington Channel and returning by the West-side of Cornwallis Island."

(I sign in great optimism, leaving behind a message with some graves and a cairn, letting the crew overhear my comments . . .)

(*Sir John Franklin commanding the Expedition* All Well)

THE ICE CLOSES

Nosing the two ships around Boothia
he cut past headlands
shrouded with rock and ice.
Whelmed by waves, a broad flotsam
cuts off the western way,
moving with an admiral's logic.

Terror and Erebus float right on down the strait,
the jagged line forms behind, sternchasing all the way.
The undiscovered passage closes on them.
Franklin knows the fangs will hold
and splinter the ships.
He bundles up and paces, eyeing the ice
all around: water space diminishes daily and
as sunlight fades the beams creak,
creak as only wood can creak when shaken
in the teeth of indifferent northern gods
within only a few miles of known and friendly waters.

A PICTURE OF FRANKLIN, 1829

Franklin looks sad
he is lost already

the distance is
(the rush upon him)
too great
no light
on the mast
will bring help

only when Lady Jane
misses him
will they search

the smudge
behind him
is the ship
Terror or Erebus
(details are faint)
or maybe only his footprint
in the snow

LOSS OF FRANKLIN

Sir John met myth sailors
flew away from the sun
he froze one winter
went north north west
passage look-out he kept
all that time.
He saw his hand cling
frozen to rigging,
saw the last seals die.
He called them Esquimaux.
Still he wouldn't float
for long in bay ice like
Boothia, McClintock Channel
and Franklin Strait,
all glaring white white
white in the map
pages carved of ice and snow
where a man, black as print
is lost
for the ships
to search the horizon
and rename the infinities.

FOOTNOTE

When in 1830 James Ross
discovered Point Victory
he named two points of land
then in sight:
Cape Franklin
and Cape Jane Franklin.

Eighteen years afterwards
Franklin's ships
perished
within sight of those headlands.

[*found poem: McClintock's*
Narrative . . . *Boston, 1860*]

14

FROZEN IN

Like living on solid ground
the ship does not move
is as safe as houses
no storm
can shake or sink it.

Winter gives us only peace
and calm
even when it blows
a gale around us.

It's not
like being a sailor
at all:
a shore leave
with no where to go.

Life aboard ship
goes on as usual.
There is no fear
among us.
When the ice melts
the ship sails out.
It is as certain
as the seasons.

The crew is always busy
scraping ice
off the railing
out of the rigging
or hunting for sport
though we have food
for years.

Every Sunday
they dance hornpipes
slapping with hard feet
the deck
in time to concertina
and mouth-organ.
They pass time in glad dance
joyed at not sweating at shrouds
hauling by hand
ships across the Pacific.

HOT RUM RATION

The amber fire of it is rationed
in life-flaming swigs
steam rises as the boiling kettle
bows to the old chipped mug.
Set on the wardroom table
steam spouts, the smell of it beckons.

Even now the crew is draining their daily jigger.
We save much fuel this way,
as Rum is better than coal
for keeping us warm
fueling our cold-stoked bodies
against the long night's chill.

Navy Rum in kegs stacked dream-high
in the dark hold below-ships:
enough rum at 3 oz. per man per day
for three years regulation swilling,
with more to fight the cold besides
stashed in the medicine chests
of the doctor and each officer
and the one I'm saving, provided by
my thoughtful Jane when we left
in case of a disaster just such as this.

Draining the rum down slow, the heat
sparks some life into my heart
unbinds for a moment the icy chain
that works toward it, the warmth spreads
out from the centre of a swallowed sun
unlimbers the lungs from their old pain
as the fumes work through the porous flesh

leaking in the glad southern sun
shining on kegs piled high at docks
cargoed out from Jamaica
where sugarcane is picked by black cubans
brought up from home across the ocean:
for it is good Navy Rum of the R.N.
served up well as a panagyric potion
sure cure for each of our day-long ills,
in this land where the days get longer.

AVOIDING DAYDREAMS

In his cabin, Franklin would lie down and kick his shoes off, feet pointed toward the writing desk. Off the deck his mind wandered freely and he would groan to himself as thoughts too dreadful burned him. At last he slept. Slept until the steward woke him, noticing as he did how the portrait of Jane was turned to the wall so Franklin in his bed could not see her face.

DREAMS IN THE LONG NIGHT

Old Sailor: In Amsterdam by god
                 there was a woman,
                 I met her in the pub
                 went crawling up
                 her steps, not too old then
                 for riding all night at anchor
                 in friendly ports, raising
                 sail, and furling it.

                 But dreaming it every night
                 now torments me, that's hell
                 that is. Without no chance
                 of her hot lips going all over,
                 and nothing here but the ice.

Young Sailor: Though young, I too, remember,
                 from my swaying hammock, how
                 in Barbados there was
                 a black woman who
                 sang softly all night
                 in a·strange tongue—
                 and in the islands
                 bare-breasted women
                 swam to us through the surf.

Old Sailor: On the deck mending yarn, we talk,
                 splicing the yarns
                 while bitches in heat
                 whine around the ship
                 where the studs chase and mount

throb their red flash
in and out while their claws
freeze to the deck:
and do they have claws, those bitches.
Boy, stay away from malamutes.

There's nothing to do about it
waking in a sweat,
and not a damn thing, lad, but
to clean it up, not a . . .

Capt. Crozier: Dream; that's all.
Sleep whenever you can.
Only the past is fleshed
in memory; climbing
steps in every new port . . .
paid off in prize-money
and full of rum too,
swaying up steps in towns
from Gibraltar to Cape Horn
finding women, dark or white,
dusky and husky-busty in ports
from the Pacific, Barbados,
and Amsterdam itself.
But here there is no woman,
none at all—

PYGMALION

While stuck in the ice we organized a sculpture
contest among the crews. A fresh fall of snow
today, and we all went out. Crozier, Fitzjames
and I to judge the results.
Two best: from Erebus a white woman carved and
curved of snow, but someone from Terror made
with coal a black one.
No words can express the futility of these men
driven to such cold procreation.

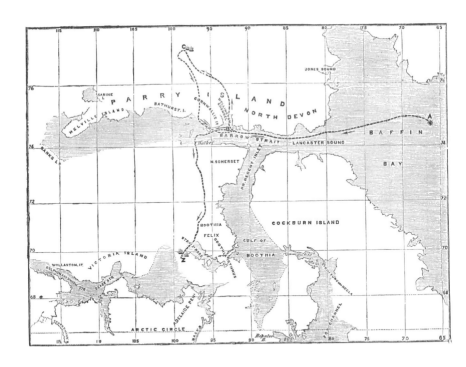

CONSTITUTIONAL

Walking with Crozier
the deck at night
passing each other
at regular intervals
our thoughts turn
on the axis
of the frozen pole
where all the ways
one looks are south;
perversely we discuss
the passage
and soon sending men
to sledge it through.

Taking another turn
we hope the ice-claws
will let us pass
that this cerberus
will remit.

Anticipating my orders
Crozier proves himself
a capable second officer
well able to command
the expedition: sure to
make himself a name.

We talk much
in revealing fragments
scattered here and there
late at night
when our moods coincide,
the rhythm of our paces
a duet.

LT. GORE SETS OUT

Franklin: An optimist I, else would not be
an explorer. Gore will find the pass.
I am an optimist. Didn't I set out
after shipwreck, bound for China Seas?

Crozier: And that was the beginning.

Franklin: And after the war:
unemployment . . . halfpay ashore.

Crozier: They were hard times.

Franklin: Exploring possibilities,
the Admiralty entered
the Arctic search.

Crozier: We couldn't refuse honourable service.

Franklin: After three years of halfpay
I was tempted: An overland trek
past the Athabasca and Great Slave.

Crozier: And that was the beginning.

Franklin: Now I am pale, shivering.

Crozier: Come, stand in the sun.

Franklin: Once I was governor of a land
in the sun. Factions condemned me

to wander far from the sun and whither.
Where is the dawn of my return?

Crozier: Do not for a moment
think of failure.

Franklin: Keep watch for Gore.

Crozier: You will know the moment
he returns.

Franklin: I go to my cabin. I am ill.
The ice is forming. Here,
and here.

Crozier: And that was the ending.

AN ORDER TO CROZIER

You must get them out.
Some have the scurvy, Crozier,
soon you must go
walking their pale flesh
out of the north.

We were desperate to come this far
huddled around a furnace stove
that had to be put out
in rough weather.

Shivering for warmth
we came, and may well stay.
I was driven to answer
foam and wind—I am a sailor yet:
my hands grip the rail
hard and tight even now
gnarled like old rope and wood
where I lean out, feet planted
with the wood stuck in the ice
making an arc to encompass it all as mine.

Others will come, Crozier, and finish.
Go and show them how:
take them a message as eternal
as the verdict this stillness
has burrowed into my heart.

DISCOVERY

So it was that when Gore and his men sledged back
from a quick dash of search and discovery they found
all quiet where the two ships canted together in
the ice. No games. No sledging.

Returning from King William's Land where he saw
the ice of Victoria Strait run without a break
all the way into Simpson, Gore surveyed the last
link of the passage; sledged into it, so close
to where Franklin had brought them.

Coming aboard Erebus he was told of Franklin, taken ill,
carried below, a pain in his heart—Gore went to him:
the pass blocked by ice was there, and if only the ice
would open, they could sail like blood through the
ventricle.

Franklin, ringed by anxious officers, closed his eyes
and carried into silence Gore's last report of success
and discovery.

1848

When three years were gone, the supplies ran out,
and England knew. The searches began, covering
21,000 miles of coast and water in 12 years.

Ross and Forsyth. Spedden in his private yacht.
Grinnel the mad American.

Between 1847 and 1851, 21 expeditions found
absolutely nothing.

1. SOMEWHERE IN THE ICE

This is the one wreck
they'll never find,
those explorers
and searchers
after my bones.

Ice coated and preserved
like pitch the rigging.
This place
is like a cave
inside the ice
where we all hide
from history.

They will never find this ship.
They want to know,
but we are well hidden
in the ice
in the memory
a fragment stored
in the cold clear brain.

2. OFF KING WILLIAM'S LAND

The deck doesn't heave:
you'd notice that right off
standing
at the useless helm
canted to port
and stern at an angle of 10°

how long it's been here
who knows,
and what ship it is.
Newly abandoned . . . or
drifting around up here
for the last 150-years?

Looking down at the ice
it is possible,
for ice is a part
of all other ice—
it is possible to see
the marks
of departing men.
They dragged small boats
across the ice—
toward the peaks that were
King William's Land
but are now
some other shore.

In the cabin . . .
my logbook stands

waiting for a last entry
before
the ghosts of men
and dogs
trek over the ice
without food
or sledges
toward the dim
island
where our bones
lie
undisturbed
except by memory
calling like seabirds
gnawing like wolves

CROZIER

we have learned
to live like Eskimos
instead of dying
    like Englishmen

we live as we can

crawling on bellies
imitating seals
in the land where the seabird's cry
is strange

We have not brought away enough from the ships;
trekking over ice hauling supplies in sledges
and small boats, using men as dogs:
so much of what we brought away
we cannot use: now I see
too late that we must travel light

I command, here on the ice.
But the ones I sent to the ship do not return:
Men and officers leave me,
some go north-east—
I will not follow them.

The loyal steward, my lieut. and I (those who remain)
must follow Back's river out,
march to Great Slave one thousand miles
and I remember young McClintock
sledging with dogs nearly that far

Now if we had dogs . . . but we have seen no eskimos,
they avoid us and will not help
and would never part with dogs,
so much like asking them for life
in this land where hopes freeze.

The wind howls tonight
around the cairn we built
piling stones one on one
at this junction of inland rivers.
We have come far
but the wind howls
and we huddle in a single tent
while the light dims and the snow
settles warm to cover our dream . . .

RAE'S REPORT:

Dr. Rae at Boothia on a Hudson's Bay Co. exploration met Esquimaux who told him of 40 white men trekking across the ice near King William's Land.

    "Crozier walked at the head of his men, all of them pulling the boat along, supplies hauled with drag ropes. They traded for seal-meat from the natives, these thin white men. He was a tall man, and they knew he was a chief because he walked by himself.

    The boat was overturned, a body underneath it. Tents and bodies. The body of the chief lay on the island a telescope strapped over his shoulders, and his gun beneath.

    The last survivors of the white men fed on dead bodies, the natives found them hacked and cut. In the kettles there was flesh.

    Some men were still alive when the Canada Geese went north in May . . . feathers on the ice and hollow bones, scattered where the men set out."

To Dr. Rae went ten thousand pounds silver, a reward from the government for his clear definition of fate.

2
McCLINTOCK
1857-1859

STEAM AND ICE

the *Fox* , steaming through icepacks
is the frontis-piece

a wood-cut
1859
black and white

the contrast of shade
definite
as the horizon
between steam
and ice

McCLINTOCK LOOKS BACK

He remembered trek ice
the morbid night of rigging

great layers
hove the bowsprit—
jerked toward Polaris:

somewhere in the earth
flows moved to cover
Sir John Franklin—
bits of metal,
oarlocks shaped to harpoon
knife, the names frozen
like marrow in the bones
a logbook
that cracked beneath his stare

ROUTES ON THE MAP

In the northwest pass
I trace the line of voyages,
across the page they are
dots for Franklin,
solid for me, McClintock

and do I feel the bite of freezing
in my fingertip? Jerk it
from the foaming
where print captures and tosses

swarms at a group of men
huddled
where I have prodded them into the storm.

STANDING WATCH

As in a childhood game
taking bottles to the eyes
and looking out
I see nothing worth recording.
Hugging the ship's rail,
perched like a pearl-diver
on his height of wood,
my balance is uncertain.
At any moment something large and white
might move in the distance.

We launch out into the ice
feeling caught in a blindfold game
whirling and twirling for position
nudging the floes with the bow.

This confrontation is eternal,
a deferred decision pending adolescence
while the whole mass slides
aslant the side: and all that splinters
is not spoiled, breaks only the ice after all.

We breathe again, ungagged, yet bound,
bluffing the ice into thinking
we are its match, not even worth
the struggle. We poke it feebly,
like the blind man with only a stick.

What is visible in the glass
is my uncertainty. Fearing it,
and watching with both eyes,
I almost see men walking
across the white fields.
Strained beyond eyesight
I pass the glass to Hobson.
Each must have his turn.

MEETING NATIVES

Whenever among the floes
we find a group of Eskimos
staked out in tents and snowhuts
waiting for winter
we talk to them.

All are friendly.
When they see us
they seem happy.
Always they share
what they have.

We talk slowly, so they will understand.
They stare back at us and say
they have seen no ships.
They understand because we talk slow.
They answer us with no lies.
They understand perfectly.

The food is hot.
Their smiles are warm.
Their smoke rises to greet us.

STOPPING FOR TEA

She is boiling us strong tea
squatting
with her thighs open to the fire
to let the warmth in
as she waits
drumming her fingers on the pot
and Petersen talks on about home
while I stare
at the olive skin of the Eskimo's wife

Strange how I feel about her
not wanting to touch
though aware of my need
of her warmth
we huddle so close to
but the chill is in her blood unlike mine
and the tea is ready
poured in my tin mug
when I recall seeing once my English
rose-bud beauty
through the fragrant steam
rising off bone-China
the tea burns
as I drink it scalding hot

McCLINTOCK AT DE ROS ISLET

Kal-lek, the only eskimo with a bald-head
and memorable for that
the old chief
has seen no ships
or wrecks drifting on his shore
he only asks
the tall British Captain
(since the reindeer have gone away)
"Will you tell us where they've gone?"
for of course, the Captain
comes in a wooden boat
and is tall and blue-eyed

ICEBERG AT MELVILLE BAY

We make the *Fox* fast to the iceberg
where ice covers
the whole bay
north into the steep
face of the glacier

having come
with no problems
along the edge
of the middle ice
it defeats us
hove-to
near the iceberg which
lies aground deep
in 58 fathoms
the cone of the peak
winking at us
spasmodically

AUGUST 12th, 1857

"The glacier serves to remind one at once of Time
and Eternity—of time, since we see portions of it
break off to drift and melt away; and of eternity
since its downward march is so extremely slow that
no change in its appearance is perceptible from
age to age."

McClintock

46

THE WINTER'S EDGE

We are well into it now.
Days grow hard.
Winter is sharpening up
against the whetstone.
I make routine notations in the log,
constantly refer to the almanac.
Soon we will be trussed up
and served on the flat bright plate.

Winter is a carving
of low ice rise and hill
in the faces of the People:
days are long and sharp.

Blades lunge at us from all sides . . .
winter spinning by
catches us early in its drift
and only opens its trap to a slice of dry sun
peeled and hung on the rim.

AUGUST 20th, 1857

"Birds have become scarce—the few we see are
returning southward. How anxiously I watch the
ice, weather, barometer and thermometer."

McClintock

THE EXPLORERS' ART

The explorers
were artists
in their way

they had an eye

quickly noted
detail
the shades
of arctic colour
they did not
paint

and although
they jotted
prose
in yellow
journals

one could not say
that they wrote

or anything else much
but
that they were here first
with their sharp
quick eyes

ALONE

loneliness
is the worst thing
forget
all that I have told you
of the colours
the rocks
the ice

snow is a blankness

hunting fills time
and stomach
fills the mind
with words
to fill the journal

writing
is only to say
what I have done

and to write
I must do
. . . anything

next to being alone
that is the worst

HUNTING ON THE ICE

-1-

Today we went hunting on the ice,
walking several miles from the *Fox*
when the weather was good.
Saw a blackbird very high.
Didn't shoot, as the dogs
thrive on fresh seal.

Carl Petersen does the hunting,
he and Christian
beat the ice—
with strange cries
they hunt
blood in their throats
the voice of
the seal
they call
beating the ice

I think they become berserk
what they hunt, seals
and the seals pop out
the hole they made
to see them waiting
like two crazy seals
and just like that
they shoot him dead
through the head as
arctic survival is perfect
and a shot in the beef
is not good
for stopping them.

I really am alone here.
Petersen and Christian
the Esquimaux
are alone here.
We are all alone
a ship . . . steam-yacht,
officers and crew.

We are an emptyness
in the emptyness.
The land does not exist—
it is a myth
frozen over
for a little while
which will soon melt
exposing
our true condition
in the world.

We drift out
and may never
adapt . . .

*
***
*

Peterson and the Esquimaux
are becoming more like seals.
Today they shot
and howled
their blood joy.

Around the ship
stuck in the ice
with snowbanks piled
to the sides
like foothills—
dogs are dancing
in grim joy
with Petersen
the hunter
and the feast of
seal blubber
from his heaven
enough for a week.

*
***
*

-3-

We drift in floe-ice.
The boundaries
must soon give way.
Our claim to this land
will melt
in the warm sea.

Perfection is an ice-crystal,
hard as light rays
in the long night
where we slip quietly through.

SLOWING

McClintock tells Hobson and Young they'll send sledges
when the ice breaks. But it's a long season.
Mist rises and hides the moon.
Caught and rattled in the teeth of the gods:
cannibal-clan festivals and totems
glow at them out of the mist.
Eyes stare from emerald masks.
The steam is their impatience, the mist
their anger.
The cards in his hand at whist fade and his fingers
blur. In the snug light of the wardroom
he notices without curiosity, noting only the fact,
how much the nails have grown, and how they curl
gently down from the finger.

LOST

Only
in our games
do we strive

at whist
Captain Young
complains
and we are too bored
to admit
the futility
of each evening's
rubber

I pretend of course
that the 13 cards
freshdealt
in my hand
are lunar months
dropping one by one
on the tricks.

This is an illusion
deeper than the world,
or so we pretend.
And the loss
of a single trick
is greater than loss.

THE BURIAL IN THE ICEPACK

Scott the enginedriver
died through the long night
in some moon
phase
overhung with auras
strange rays that fix
a deeper dark in visible form

he tripped in a dark hold

cutting through ice
to make a sea burial
I perform
the solemn rite
stare into the pit
white walls, foot-thick
and dark waters
that wait

complacent
the body on a sledge,
covered with the union jack

spars stand like crosses
against haloes of moonlight

NO LAND

Around the ship
is no man's land
no land for men
or animals

even the birds fly
high
and descend
only when they
must
or to fish
the slate waters
or to rest

who would live here
unless
they were forced to settle
who would want the land
who would be a pioneer?

when I leave,
only bones
will remain
I will take
the relics
my book of notes
my wooden boat
and go
for I have seen the best parts
and more truth in that
for the best parts
are unsettling and therefore
unsettled

DOGWATCH

On the calm nights
the dogs charge
up the snow banks
piled to the deck
and break like waves
all along the ship

whenever the binnacle light
goes out—
"Why, bless you, sir
they makes a regular sortee
and in they all comes."

Repelling borders
in nightshirts and broomsticks
the crew chases
dogs Dogs DOGS
around the deck,
swatting
DOGS out of every nook
they get in,
missing sleep
for the fun
of repelling Dogs—
but it takes only two hours
of the dogwatch
to drive them
back to the ice,
and to hell off'n the ship.

DREAM IN THE LONG NIGHT

we take meals
by lamplight
now the sun
is gone
for the year

the dogs rush
and howl to glimpse
the moon

breaking our sleep
in dream
fragments
where the ship
rolls
on an open sea

BREAKUP

I've been in the crow's nest eyeing all day
as heaves and cracks spring the ice.
Open lanes run within 100 yards of the ship,
and close by next day.
The pack breaks around us
making it dangerous
to be here
as it drifts past Disco coast
into warmer waters
that wear it out
with sounds like axes falling.
I balanced here eight hours
today, watching.
We run clear, then drift,
squeezed by frigid muscles.
We are again a ship,
as the pack rolls,
resumes the function of an ocean.

SECOND ATTEMPT

After refitting in Greenland the *Fox*
plows the bow through the sea
dropping seeds
of exploration and search.
Turned back the first season
time is more valuable now.
The nose meets ice in each bay.
Turned away by
the gods of the blizzard,
who drifted us ingloriously out,
ship shaking in storm.
We could not comprehend
such anger.
          The whalers
tell us where to take on coal:
the captains add provisions
to our store. Also fresh fruit.
The *Fox* is set
to run the field
and plunge full length
past snares
fast at last
to be caught in ice
and held one more winter
closer the objective.

Once frozen in, the ship
becomes a base for search—
the sledges, men and dogs
blossom out over the ice
to plant with ice-runners
the straight lines of our coming.

MONUMENT

At the entrance
to Barrow Strait
we set
the marble
by hand
to spot
Franklin's last winter.

I cannot read
the words.
They set
too close—
waver
on the monument.

For Lady Franklin,
we stowed it
through a winter
to where
they set out
for science
and country:
for those
who did not return
we bring
the headstone.

WINTER QUARTERS

it must have been like this
at first with Franklin,
one at at time, death in his party.
Night is icebound,
time will not move—
it is a force
slow and austere

In November Mr. Brand,
who worked the engines
after Scott, apoplexy took him.
No engineer or driver,
just 2 stokers, 24 of us left
including interpreter and 2
Greenland Esquimaux

temperature dropping to -31°

causing ice cracks across the harbour
we're come to Bellot Strait, in parties,
set at depots, and into winter quarters

and wait
bound by cold spells, hunting—
Our Esquimaux, Samuel, shot a fawn today.

HOBSON CROSSES THE ICE

Lt. Hobson sledges out and back.
He is the first to go into the dark.
But returns from only latitude 71½°
when the sea beating cliffs
ended the smooth run
of his road to the north.
Hobson is well and young
and will soon throw off
the scurvy from his long trip
with men and sledges
and little food,
carrying for warmth
only his fire inside.

McCLINTOCK, SLEDGING

Sledging for days, Petersen and I.
No sight of natives.
They winter this far north;
but we have found none.
  The problem is, we
  look only ahead.

Petersen calls to me to look
and four men
are walking after us.
So great was our joy that
we immediately
buckled on revolvers
and advanced to meet them.
Hunters returning home;
we joined them.
          And paying
each man a needle,
they built for us a snowhut
to rest a night.

We see before long
one Esquimaux wears
a Navy button
and ask him how it came—

"It came from white men
starved where there are salmon."
He did not understand
how it could happen
with food so available.

But he had been to the island
to salvage their wood and iron.

We talked about it all night
Petersen and I until the whole
village of People appeared.
Trade commenced but Petersen
could not obtain
the fine native dogs we wanted.

A man, old from living
in this land, not from age,
told his name: Ooblooria.

Halting for his words to catch up
he made it clear:
No people saw the whites.
They died.
One saw their bones.
Some were buried.

The ones on the island
are dead.
The bones are there.
The others . . . how could
they live?
If you think they crossed the
the ice, follow them.
None here know more
than this.

It was then that Petersen ran
from the trading, came up to me
puffing blue steam—

"That man, he knows. .He was there."

So the natives told us
what they would:
a ship with three masts
crushed in the ice—
bones in the spring.

Sledging back to the *Fox*
we were pounds lighter,
eating only
seal blubber carved in
wafers,
but we were ready to search
to travel and retrieve
the ruins
of wood & iron.

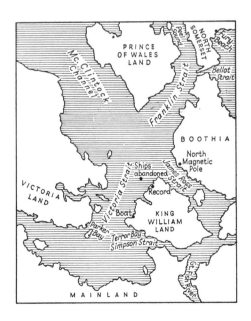

HEALING

The days are getting longer
time stretches a bit
between the hours.
The fabric yields and gapes like gauze.
I lie back uncaring and rest for the journey,
tired still, but impatient for news.
I have sent Hobson out again
to search the coast
and find what he can.
When rested I will follow
with Petersen the path he has gone.
Maybe tomorrow the muscles
will be still, the fluids replenished.
I drink much tea while waiting
and soon we shall go.
The days are now far too long
stretching the nerves too thin;
we stuff the tiny cracks that appear
with canned-beef water and warmth;
we stitch slowly the seams together
and pluck out one at a time
the needles our scurvy left in the flesh.

FRANKLIN'S BURIAL

Without hesitation,
the dream centres
where a native remembered him

laughed as harpoon glanced
off frozen boulders
bled water
crystal and white split
the stone

long after
the last dog was eaten
and the fleas frozen
and the wished for flame
only a petrified lamp
stuck in the ice

with other belongings—
frozen names, oars,
the spars of a boat
their rings cast around the bones

SKELETONS AND RELICS: McCLINTOCK, May 1859

Like a page
brittle and melting
the snowflakes one
by one they fall
as we make our list of
skeletons and relics
in this boat from 'Erebus'
> *2 skeletons, skulls missing*
> *6 tracts and the 'Vicar of Wakefield'*
> *tea and chocolate (40 pounds of the latter)*

the ink in my pen
seems frozen, slow
like tree sap in winter
> *portion of tobacco in pemmican tin marked E*
> *5 watches*
> > hands fixed pointing eternity

Gravedigging in ice is hard work
it can't be done on tea and chocolate
no wonder there are only two skeletons
the rest gnawed by wolves—dragged away

> *"Of the many men, probably twenty or thirty, who*
> *were attached to this boat,*
> *it seemed most strange*
> *that the remains of only two individuals were*
> > *discovered . . ."*

One alone in the bow
disturbed by wolves,
the other in back surrounded by
  11 large spoons
  11 forks
  04 teaspoons
 all of silver, eight Franklin's
others marked with officer's crests.
Did the unmarked fork, the three
items marked with an owl
 belong to these?

No matter, they lie here
oblivious,
 a viking burial scene, plunder
at their feet
  the monument protects them
   "two double barrel guns—one barrel in each
  loaded and cocked—
   standing muzzle upward
   against the boat's side . . ."

THE CAIRN

(McCLINTOCK, May, 1859)

Stone by stone Lt.
Hobson tore it down to the ground
of the island.
Crozier's notes snug there,
preserved in a tin.
              We made
copies. Rebuilt the cairn
with the record sealed.
Left a record to guard
our discovery against
failure to return.

The note:
           "Franklin died today",
is where the page creased
when it thawed.

That left Crozier drifting,
commander of the ice.

One ship crushed:
Franklin died through
the long winter,
and the ship
was buried alive
in the pack
when the last summer
brought no warmth.

The claw
of earth
did not melt.

And the natives only say:
Out in the sea
to the west
of King William's Land
a ship with three masts
was eaten by the ice,
all the people landed safely.

The natives
obtained from her, nothing.

Later they picked
from the scatter of death
the relics
that lead us
like the bones of saints,
providing as signs
the harpoon-spear
shaped from the boat
and a button
from a castaway coat.

A record, maddening
in official brevity
tells not even between the lines
what happened when they stopped
to pile the stones for a cairn.
What it says is so silent:
water scrawling rocks in lines of sand,
that it is not certain
what meaning they piled
in the rock,
or what happened
to the men who moved the stones.

"OH, TO BE IN ENGLAND . . ."

Frozen about as numb as Franklin
it's hard to be joyous or cheerful
but I am
when at last I stand
where Franklin stood,
having at hand relics of his.
I hold in mind
the hard coming to here
and hold also
the knowledge of his fate.
Here in the North
at the tag-end of winter
I feel
the sap of trees somewhere
stirring
to end the pain
the news taken all at once
like medicine
in sad celebration;
tired but trudging homeward
we move as into a new season.

A SHIP

An old woman says
it drifted up and broke
the natives found
a body aboard
they say
they found
no one alive.

They saw nothing themselves.
They know nothing.
They did not help.
Always it was someone else.

AFTER THE VOYAGE . . .

McClintock went home again
and all his crew
went back to songbirds in meadows
and parks where tame deer
nibble the grass quite short.

After working into the land's heart
and way of thought
their ship lay like an embolism
in the mighty works.
Each built in his soul
a dam against the flood
that burst—
tossed them on the foam by day
and on heavy seas at night
until they reached home
shaken up but still alive
and sane enough
to huddle in port
warmed by lamps
in the industrial heart
blazing about them.

They were put off by the stillness
by infinite peace
that turned them in upon themselves
to explore.
When they had the opportunity
to know themselves
they devised diversions
and let it die.

Only by beginning at the base
and moving
on at the right time
having subdued the land
and themselves
could they reach the passage
and come out transfigured
from East to West.

When they most had the land
they let it go.
Left it instead to lie in the long night
while Eskimos hunted north
after caribou herds
and star light
traced the old patterns after them
unshadowed
by any destiny but their own . . .

MYTH

Never forget Franklin and McClintock
let mythmakers spin tales
fine as barometer strands
(human hair)
but take them as they are
visitors

who on the way reindeer
and muskoxen discovered
left behind relics
boat spars, the subtle
shades of experience
in Samuel the hunter's mind—
bullets in the skulls of animals

and sledge tracks
that once sang along the snow
closing with a line
the points between silence & night